Battleground Europe
WATERLOO
The Battlefield Guide

Andrew Uffindell
and
Michael Corum

LEO COOPER

First published in Great Britain in 2003
and reprinted in 2015 by
PEN & SWORD MILITARY
An imprint of
Pen & Sword Books Ltd
47 Church Street
Barnsley
South Yorkshire, S70 2AS

ISBN 978 0 85052 878 7

A CIP catalogue record for this book is
available from the British Library.

Printed and bound in England
By CPI Group (UK) Ltd, Croydon, CR0 4YY

Pen & Sword Books Ltd incorporates the imprints of Aviation, Atlas,
Family History, Fiction, Maritime, Military, Discovery, Politics, History,
Archaeology, Select, Wharncliffe Local History, Wharncliffe True Crime,
Military Classics, Wharncliffe Transport, Leo Cooper, The Praetorian Press,
Remember When, Seaforth Publishing and Frontline Publishing.

For a complete list of Pen & Sword titles please contact
PEN & SWORD BOOKS LIMITED
47 Church Street, Barnsley, South Yorkshire, S70 2AS, England
E-mail: enquiries@pen-and-sword.co.uk
Website: www.pen-and-sword.co.uk

CONTENTS

Singular Gallantry of an Officer of the Imperial Guards.
Published by J. Robins Dec'r 26 1816.

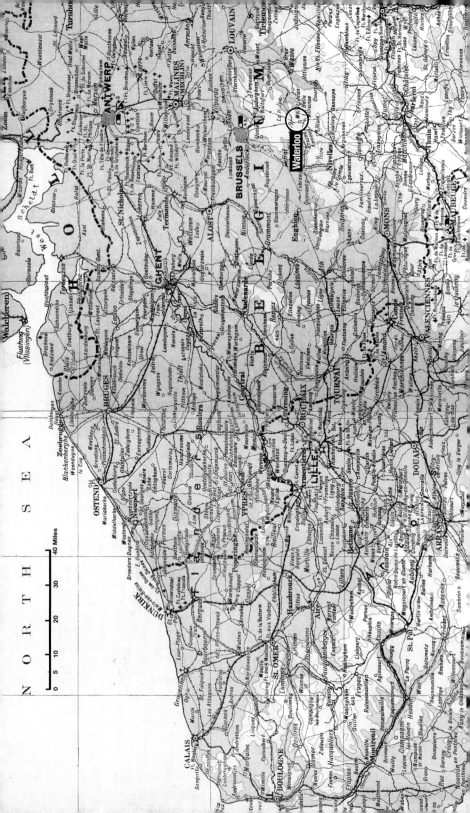

INTRODUCTION

The aftermath of Waterloo sickened everyone. As one British officer remarked, the battlefield was so strewn with carnage that 'it seemed as if the world had tumbled to pieces, and three-fourths of everything was destroyed in the wreck.'

The battle marked the climax of four extraordinary months. Napoleon Bonaparte, Emperor of the French, had been defeated and exiled following two decades of war. In March 1815, however, he slipped back to the southern coast of France, marched on Paris and swiftly regained power from the unpopular King Louis XVIII.

Aghast at his dramatic reappearance, the European powers prepared for war and soon formed a formidable coalition comprising Austria, Prussia, Russia, Great Britain, Portugal, Spain, Sweden and some minor German states.

But the allies would not be ready to invade France until the summer and that enabled Napoleon to launch a pre-emptive strike against the United Netherlands, an amalgamated Belgium and Holland under Dutch rule. Two allied armies were assembling here: a Prussian army under Field Marshal Gebhard Leberecht von Blücher and the Duke of Wellington's composite army cobbled together with contingents from Britain, the United

Napoleon on his return from exile rapidly won over the French army as he marched on Paris. (ASKB)

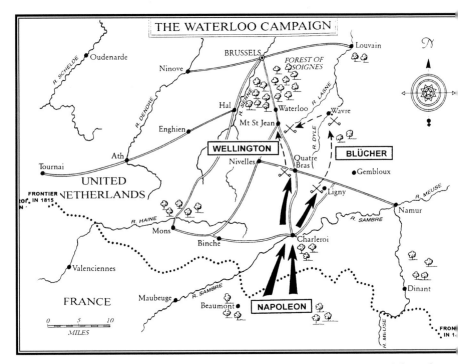

THE WATERLOO CAMPAIGN

Netherlands and the German states of Hanover, Brunswick and
Nassau.

Between them, Wellington and Blücher had 210,000 men
against Napoleon's strike force of 124,000, but had to disperse
them over a wide area to cover all the potential invasion routes.
Napoleon therefore launched a surprise attack on 15 June at the
junction of the two allied armies in the hope of destroying them
piecemeal. Next day, he dealt the Prussians a serious but
inconclusive defeat at the Battle of Ligny, twenty-six miles south-
east of Brussels. Wellington, who was still concentrating his army,
was meanwhile contained by part of the French army under
Marshal Ney at the crossroads of Quatre Bras, eight miles to the
north-west.

A lull followed on the 17th as Blücher's battered Prussians
withdrew twelve miles northwards to regroup around the town of
Wavre. Wellington likewise fell back, along a parallel route, to a
new position on the ridge of Mont St Jean, two-and-a-half miles
south of a village called Waterloo. Napoleon personally followed
Wellington with most of his army, having detached 32,000 men
under Marshal Emmanuel de Grouchy to chase the Prussians.

Wellington decided to give battle at Waterloo with the support
of Blücher, who promised to join him after leaving a rearguard at

Wavre. In the great battle that ensued on Sunday, 18 June, Wellington repelled a succession of French attacks, but took appalling losses. As one of his men remarked, 'I had never yet heard of a battle in which everybody was killed; but this seemed likely to be an exception, as all were going by turns.' Late in the afternoon, the first Prussian troops arrived on the eastern edge of the battlefield and entered the fray, to be reinforced by more and more of their comrades. As dusk fell, the exhausted and outnumbered French army finally collapsed and fled the field. Napoleon abdicated as Emperor four days later and by the end of October was back in exile, this time on the lonely, South Atlantic island of St Helena, where he died in 1821.

Waterloo was one of the great, decisive battles of history, ending over twenty years of war and opening an extraordinary era of peace. Not until the Crimean war of 1854-6 did another major conflict break out and by then new weapons were being produced that would drastically alter the face of warfare, making Waterloo one of the last battles in which troops wore colourful uniforms and fought in tightly-packed ranks. For the British, Waterloo has a particular significance because it marked the dawn of their imperial glory and was the last time that they fought the French.

Despite the passage of time, Waterloo has lost none of its fascination and over three hundred thousand people from all over the world visit the battlefield every year. So come with us to tour this remarkable site and see where history was made.

Inniskilling Dragoons see to their horses and prepare a meal on the eve of the Battle of Waterloo.

The Duke of Wellington accepts a hot drink from a soldier of the 1st Battalion 95th Rifles on the morning of the battle.

Napoleon reviews his army as it forms up on the morning of Waterloo. On the left is a detachment of his cuirassiers, heavy cavalrymen equipped with helmets and plates of armour to protect their chests and backs. (ASKB)

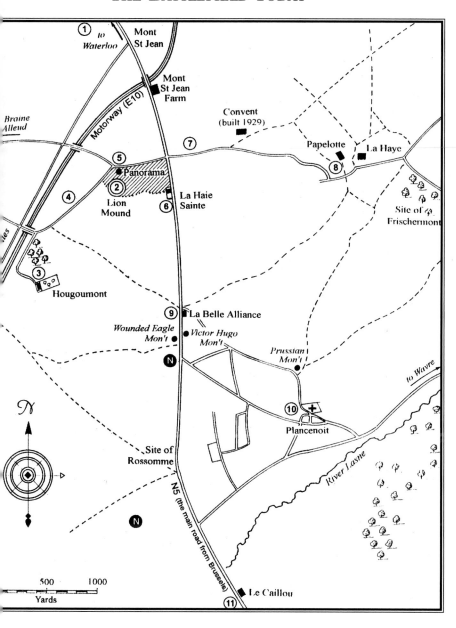

Napoleon surveys the battlefield in the evening.

BATTLEFIELD GUIDE

We recognise that you are probably on a day trip to Waterloo and have designed this tour to take you anything between a half-day and a day, depending on how much time you want to spend at each of the eleven points of interest. But if you are a history buff and want to explore the battlefield and the surrounding area in detail, you can profitably spend at least a week.

Although you will find good hotels locally, you will probably prefer to stay in Brussels, just twelve miles to the north. To reach the battlefield from Brussels, simply drive southwards along the main road called the N5. (If you do not have a car, catch a train from Bruxelles Midi station, or a bus from the Place Rouppe). The N5 runs across the battlefield, but first brings you to the town of Waterloo, where you should stop for an hour to visit Wellington's headquarters.

WELLINGTON'S HEADQUARTERS

At the time of the battle, Waterloo was a small village with fewer than 2000 inhabitants. It saw no fighting because the battlefield was two-and-a-half miles further south, but gave its name to the battle as it contained Wellington's headquarters. It has since increased its population to over 25,000 and expanded southwards right up to the northern edge of the battlefield.

The inn that served as Wellington's headquarters stands in the centre of the town, alongside the N5, and is now a museum full of fascinating exhibits, including a captured French cannon. You will also be able to trace the history of the town from prehistoric to modern times and locate the many places around the world that were named after the battle.

Wellington returned here late on the evening of the 18th after defeating Napoleon. Numbed by exhaustion, he ate a lonely supper and then, realising

The Duke of Wellington. (ASKB)

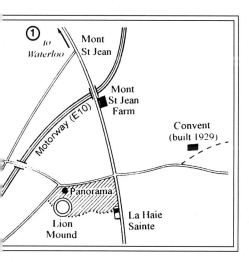

13

The village of Waterloo on the day after the battle. Note the Royal Chapel on the right; Wellington established his headquarters on the opposite side of the road. (ASKB)

Memorial plaques inside the Church of St Joseph, adjoining the Royal Chapel.

Wellington on the battlefield of Waterloo. In the background is the farm of La Haie Sainte.

how narrowly he had survived the hail of shot, suddenly exclaimed: 'the hand of Almighty God has been upon me this day.' He had to sleep that night on a pallet because one of his ADCs, Lieutenant-Colonel the Hon. Sir Alexander Gordon, lay dying in his bed; the next morning he broke down and wept as a doctor read the awful list of his casualties. He then began his despatch to Lord Bathurst, the Secretary of State for the War Department, to

Wellington's headquarters in the town of Waterloo.

announce the victory to those at home in Britain. He kept it brief and to the point, as was his habit, but caused considerable controversy by failing to give enough praise to deserving regiments and individuals. The despatch was entrusted to an ADC, Major the Hon. Henry Percy, who reached London on the evening of 21 June, three days after the battle. Such was the speed at which news travelled in those days.

As you tour the museum, you will begin to understand Wellington's brilliance as a commander, in particular his mastery of tactics, eye for the ground and insistence on seeing to as much as possible in person. 'The real reason why I succeeded in my own campaigns is because I was always on the spot,' he explained. 'I saw everything and did everything for myself.' Throughout the battle, he rode along his front line and often assumed personal

'The real reason why I succeeded in my own campaigns is because I was always on the spot.'

command of a battalion when there was a crisis. He enjoyed the trust of his men to such an extent that a battalion commander, when asked whether he had been at all anxious about the outcome of Waterloo, replied:

'Oh no, except for the Duke. We had a notion that while he was there nothing could go wrong.'

Opposite the museum stands the domed Royal Chapel, which dates from 1690. If you go through it, you enter the adjoining Church of St Joseph, which was enlarged after the battle, and inside you will find scores of memorial tablets to those who fell in the short but bloody campaign.

THE LION MOUND

N ow return to your car and drive to the battlefield itself where you will soon spot the world famous Lion Mound monument at the centre of Wellington's front line. This enormous artificial hill was erected in the 1820s, with a column of masonry in the middle supporting a statue of a lion made from twenty-eight tonnes of cast iron. It commemorates the allied victory over Napoleon and marks the spot where Prince William of Orange, one of Wellington's corps commanders and the heir to the Dutch throne, was wounded in the evening of the battle.

The lion, symbol of both the Netherlands and Britain, rests one paw on a globe and stares defiantly towards France. Unfortunately, the earth to form the monument was taken from

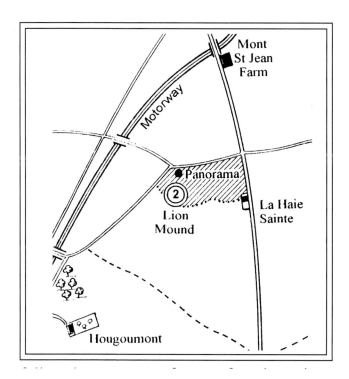

An early photograph of the battlefield of Waterloo. The mound with the lion was constructed with earth taken from the battlefield, which resulted in a change of terrain in the immediate area. The monument in the foreground is to the Hanoverians and was erected in 1818 by surviving officers. The fluted half-column commemorates the death of Lieutenant-Colonel Gordon, aide-de-camp to Wellington. This unfortunate officer after being mortally wounded was taken to Wellington's headquarters.

A modern view from the Hanoverian monument looking westwards across the Brussels road to the Gordon monument and the Lion Mound.

part of the actual battlefield, between the Mound itself and the N5, and this drastically altered the terrain here.

You can park at the foot of the Mound, where you will find a Visitors' Centre, a cluster of restaurants and souvenir shops and even a waxworks museum depicting the foremost generals of the three armies. All these buildings date from after the battle.

Before touring the battlefield, you will want to obtain a good view of it by climbing the two hundred and twenty-six steps to the top of the Mound. To gain access, you will need to go through the Visitors' Centre, where a preliminary audio-visual presentation will explain how the battle unfolded.

Overview of the battlefield

The summit of the Mound offers a spectacular view of the battlefield from a height of one hundred and thirty-five feet. You can easily follow the sequence of events from here since the terrain, except in the south-east, is protected by Belgian Law and remains largely unchanged.

Wellington's front line ran all along the ridge crest on either side of the Mound. Reserves stood further back, while out in front some fortified strongholds helped to anchor the position. These were the farms of Hougoumont in the west and La Haie Sainte in the centre and, at the eastern end of the line, the farms of Papelotte, La Haye and Frischermont and the village of Smohain.

You might wish to glance through the rest of this guide and try to identify some of the locations that we suggest you visit later. If you have a compass, you can locate the following points from the top of the Mound (all bearings magnetic azimuths):

• **Hougoumont** (Point Three) is easily spotted 1200 yards away almost due south-west (221°).

• **La Haie Sainte** (Point Six) is only 500 yards east by south-east (106°).

• **Papelotte** (Point Eight) is roughly east by north-east (86°), about 1600 yards away.

• **Plancenoit village** (Point Ten) is south-east (140°), 2800 yards in the distance.

• **La Belle Alliance** (Point Nine) is south by south-east (156°), 1300 yards away.

The first thing to strike you about the battlefield is how small it is: all the major fighting took place in roughly five square miles.

Wellington

Crossroads

Wellington's Eastern Wing Point 7

Pape Poi

Brussels

Gordon Monument

Hanoverian Monument

Ground taken to form the Lion Mour

Looking east from the Lion Mound.

Keep in mind throughout your tour how this contributed to the intensity of the carnage.

Note, too, that the main feature of the ground is the valley that runs roughly east-west between the positions of the two armies: Wellington held the ridge on the northern side and to attack him, the French had to cross this exposed valley and then move uphill to reach his lines. Waterloo was to be what Wellington called a 'pounding match' - a straightforward frontal assault on his heavily defended position. There were no outflanking moves and you can see why from where you stand. Over to the east, around Papelotte, sunken roads and relatively steep slopes made it difficult for large bodies of troops to move anywhere quickly. If you look to the west, you will see that the terrain is more conducive to movement. Wellington feared that he might be outflanked here and had therefore left a detachment of 17,000 men at the town of Hal, eight miles to the north-west, with other units nearer the battlefield at Braine-l'Alleud. In the event, Napoleon did not attempt such a move, as it would have taken too much time and would have left Marshal Grouchy's detachment dangerously isolated as it shadowed the Prussians away to the

La Haie Sainte
Point 6

Napoleon's initial positions

Napoleon

La Belle Alliance

east. Thus, Waterloo would be simply a series of frontal attacks by Napoleon against the heart of Wellington's line.

How the battle unfolded

During the morning of 18 June, Napoleon deployed his troops in a gently curving line facing Wellington three-quarters of a mile away on the other side of the valley. Each army was roughly 70,000 men strong, but Napoleon had more guns and more experienced troops. Wellington had to stiffen his line by interspersing his British and other units as he could not rely on the steadiness of some of his Dutch–Belgian and German soldiers.

Bear in mind that for the first part of the battle, the Prussians were out of sight to the east and north-east. Napoleon was unaware of exactly where they were and had no inkling that they were marching to join Wellington. Hence his plan was simply to smash through Wellington's eastern wing and then wheel round to drive the remnants of his army from the field before marching northwards to occupy Brussels. Wellington's aim was purely defensive. Until his Prussian allies joined him in overwhelming

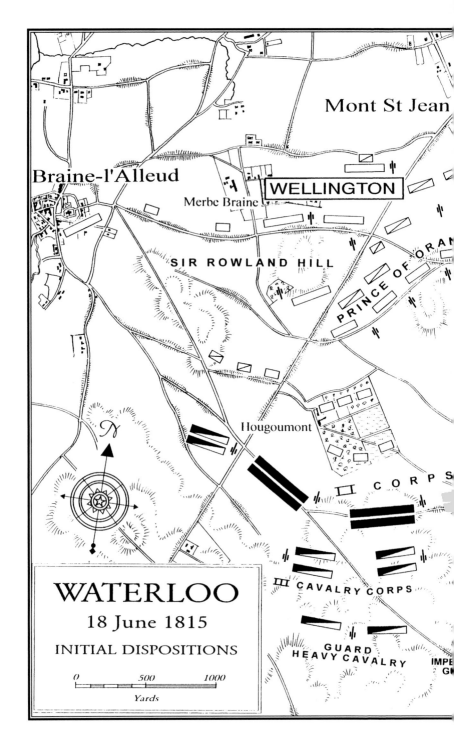

Mont St Jean

Braine-l'Alleud

WELLINGTON

Merbe Braine

SIR ROWLAND HILL

PRINCE OF ORAN

Hougoumont

CORPS

CAVALRY CORPS

GUARD
HEAVY CAVALRY

IMPE
G

WATERLOO

18 June 1815

INITIAL DISPOSITIONS

N

0   500   1000

Yards

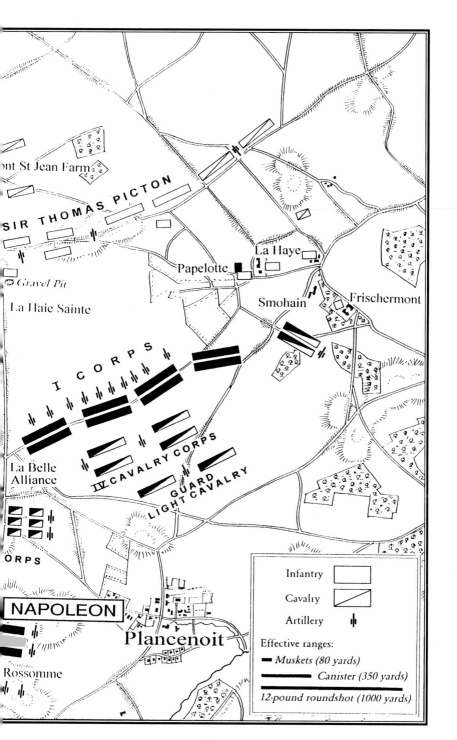

Mont St Jean Farm

SIR THOMAS PICTON

Gravel Pit

La Haie Sainte

Papelotte

La Haye

Smohain

Frischermont

I CORPS

IV CAVALRY CORPS

GUARD
LIGHT CAVALRY

La Belle
Alliance

ORPS

NAPOLEON

Plancenoit

Rossomme

Infantry	
Cavalry	
Artillery	ᚻ

Effective ranges:

━━ Muskets (80 yards)

━━━━ Canister (350 yards)

━━━━━━ 12-pound roundshot (1000 yards)

strength, he could only react to, and counter, each successive French attack.

Torrential rain during the night had turned the ground into a quagmire. Napoleon had to postpone the start of the battle, which finally began at 11.30 am when French infantry attacked the farm of Hougoumont in the west. This was only a preliminary and towards 2.00 pm, Napoleon unleashed his main assault in the eastern sector, after a heavy artillery bombardment of Wellington's ridge. French troops attempted to storm the farm of La Haie Sainte, while further east, massive infantry columns marched across the valley, only to be routed by a spectacular counter-attack of British heavy cavalry.

BATTLE OF WATERLOO: 11.30AM - 3.00PM

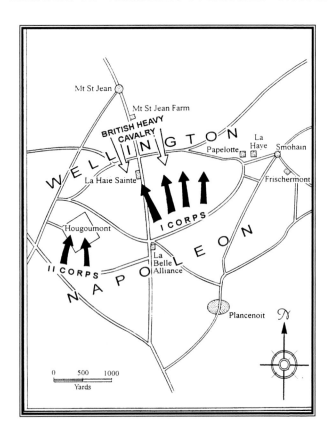

A pause ensued as the two sides regrouped. At 3.30 pm, the French made a second vain attempt to seize La Haie Sainte. Then Marshal Ney led forward masses of French cavalry to assail Wellington's centre in a series of famous charges. These lasted for an hour-and-a-half, but failed to break Wellington's line, as Ney forgot until too late to order up French infantry in support.

At 4.30 pm, the situation dramatically worsened for Napoleon. Three hours earlier, he had spotted Prussian forces five miles away through his telescope as they marched on his eastern flank. Now they finally arrived on the battlefield and assaulted the village of Plancenoit, forcing him to detach units from his reserves to try and check them. Napoleon's battle line was now

BATTLE OF WATERLOO: 3.00PM - 8.00PM

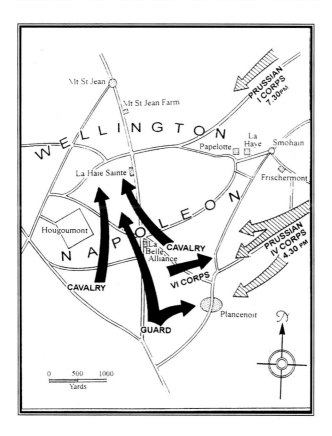

The moment of victory. Wellington, on horseback to the left, watches his army advancing into the valley. The farm of La Haie Sainte is in the middle distance.

bent back at right angles, for at the same time as his forces were attacking Wellington in the north, they were desperately trying to contain the Prussians in the east.

Towards 6.00 pm, the French finally captured La Haie Sainte and quickly exploited their success with a renewed onslaught on Wellington's front line. This time, they pushed forward a combination of infantry, cavalry and artillery acting in close mutual support. The action quickly deteriorated into a murderous attritional struggle, with Wellington's centre being torn to shreds by swarms of French skirmishers and by guns firing at close range. At this stage, Napoleon had his most experienced troops, the crack Imperial Guard infantry, still in reserve. But he did not dare commit them against Wellington's wavering line until he had contained the Prussians, who looked likely to break through in

the east at any moment. Without the help of the Guard, the
French troops attacking Wellington were unable to maintain the
pressure and fell back into the valley to regroup. A lull followed,
enabling Wellington to shore up his centre with the last of his
reserves.

Napoleon meanwhile counter-attacked the Prussians and
eventually hurled them back. This belatedly freed him to send six
Guard battalions against Wellington's centre in a final, desperate
bid to break through. But the Guard was smashed by the deadly
fire of Wellington's infantry and flung back into the valley. This
unexpected repulse coincided with the arrival of powerful
Prussian reinforcements and the demoralised French army
suddenly disintegrated into a mob of fugitives. Wellington's troops
now left the ridge that they had defended all day and advanced
southwards across the valley, while the Prussians swept in from
the east and then pursued the French into the night.

Marshal Michel Ney, Napoleon's chief subordinate at Waterloo. Dubbed the 'bravest of the brave,' he was a man of such reckless courage that he had at least five horses shot beneath him as he led the French attacks during the battle. (ASKB)

HOUGOUMONT

O nce you have seen the battlefield from the Lion Mound, go back down the steps in order to follow the fighting on ground level. We suggest that you first explore Wellington's position on foot, starting in the west, at the farm of Hougoumont, and working your way eastwards. Later, if you have time to spare, you can drive to the other side of the valley to see Napoleon's sector and the area where Blücher's Prussians fought in the afternoon.

Once you reach the foot of the Mound, therefore, take the road that runs to the south-west along the crest of Wellington's ridge and just before it goes over a motorway, turn left on to a minor road to reach the farm of Hougoumont. Situated five hundred yards in front of the ridge crest, Hougoumont anchored and protected the western end of Wellington's line. It was so important a strongpoint that it was garrisoned by some of his best troops: British Guardsmen, supported by detachments of German infantry.

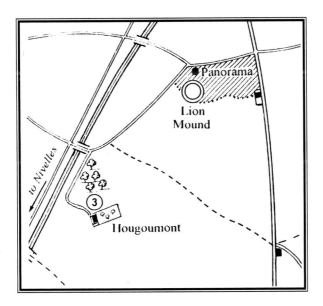

HOUGOUMONT

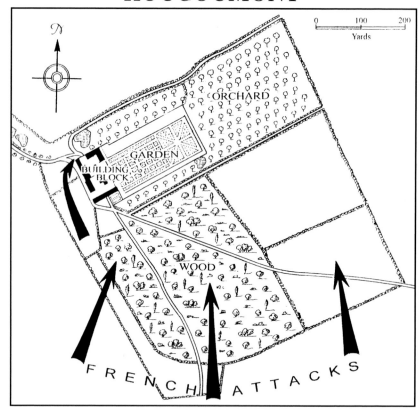

Before you stands the northern face of the building block, which formed the heart of this formidable post. If you enter through the north gateway, you will see how the buildings are grouped around a courtyard and connected by high walls to form an unbroken defensive perimeter. But remember that these buildings occupied only the north-western corner of Hougoumont, whose extensive grounds covered an area six hundred yards wide and six hundred long. Adjoining the building block to the east was a formal garden, protected on the southern and eastern sides by a loopholed wall; further east was a large orchard, while to the south stood an extensive wood. Both the wood and the orchard have since disappeared.

It was at Hougoumont that the battle began at 11.30 am and fighting continued to rage here for the rest of the day. The farm was attacked by units of the French II Corps under General

Honoré Reille, which had been drawn up four hundred yards to the south to form Napoleon's western wing. Reille entrusted the first assault to one of his divisional commanders, Prince Jérôme Bonaparte, Napoleon's headstrong youngest brother. Napoleon initially intended only a limited assault, a mere preliminary to the main attack that would strike Wellington's eastern wing early that afternoon. But such was the fervour of the French troops that they soon became embroiled in an all-out attempt to take the farm. Wellington fed in reinforcements throughout the day, but in a controlled manner. The French assaults, in contrast, escalated wildly and sucked in masses of infantry who could have been used more profitably elsewhere. In fact, the garrison of 3500 British and German troops tied down as many as 9000 Frenchmen.

The farm, which witnessed some horrific scenes, is one of the most evocative corners of the battlefield. Plaques on the farm walls pay tribute to the Coldstream and the 3rd (later

French infantry attack the Gardener's House on the southern face of Hougoumont. (ASKB)

The same scene today.

Led by Lieutenant-Colonel Macdonell, British guardsmen heave shut the North Gate moments after a handful of French troops broke into courtyard. (ASKB)

Scots) Guards, who formed the backbone of the defence, as well as two companies of the 1st (later Grenadier) Guards, who helped to defend the orchard. Another memorial commemorates the Royal Waggon Train, which kept the garrison supplied with vital ammunition.

If you go round the western side of the building block to the southern face, you can see the farm from the point of view of the French attackers. Note the memorial plaque on the corner of the garden wall to General Pierre-François Bauduin, a French brigade commander killed during the first assaults. To reach this point, the French first had to fight their way through the wood that used to stand in the southern half of the grounds and which was infested with green-coated German infantry firing from behind the trees. *'Le feu de l'ennemi était si vif et si dru,'* complained a French general. *'Le bois d'Hougoumont nous était funeste.'* ('The fire of the enemy was so sharp and heavy. For us the wood was a death trap.')

The wood extended up to about thirty yards of the garden wall, leaving a strip of open ground that had to be crossed under a hail of fire from the British and German troops holding the garden and building block. The French infantry were shot down in swathes as they vainly tried to reach and scale the wall. Those that survived the slaughter fell back to the cover of the trees, but Wellington, on the ridge crest to the north, ordered Captain Robert Bull's howitzer battery to lob shrapnel shells over the heads of the garrison and on to the luckless French troops in the wood, forcing them temporarily to evacuate it.

The French poured in more infantry and renewed the assault. A handful of their troops, led by a gigantic, axe-wielding officer nicknamed *l'Enfonceur*, 'The Smasher', stormed round the western side of the building block, broke through the North Gate and burst into the courtyard.

Lieutenant-Colonel James Macdonell, the senior British officer on the scene, gathered some men and heaved shut the gates before more Frenchmen could enter. Those trapped inside were quickly killed or captured. It was a close call, so close that Wellington himself later said that 'the success of the battle ... turned upon the closing of the gates of Hougoumont.' Bear in mind that the walls here are now much lower than they were at the time of the battle.

An old photograph of the chapel.

Hougoumont Farm in 1815

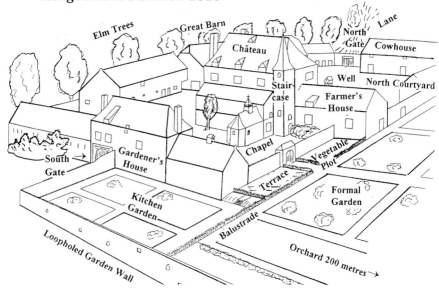

Hougoumont Farm present day

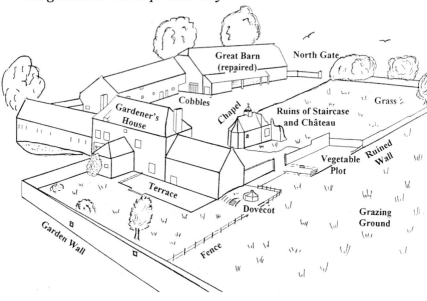

In the afternoon, Napoleon belatedly tried to destroy the stubborn garrison by ordering his howitzers to shell the farm. Many of the buildings were soon on fire and several horses and wounded men perished horribly in the flames, but Hougoumont defiantly held out. Wellington watched the inferno from the ridge to the north and calmly scribbled this message to the garrison:

I see that the fire has communicated from the Hay Stack to the Roof of the Chateau. You must however still keep your Men in those parts to which the fire does not reach. Take care that no Men are lost by the falling in of the Roof, or floors: after they will have fallen in occupy the Ruined walls inside of the Garden; particularly if it should be possible for the Enemy to pass through the Embers in the Inside of the House.

In the middle of the courtyard, you will see a little chapel, which miraculously survived the fire that gutted a large château that adjoined it. If you go inside, you will find a crucifix on the wall and will see where the flames charred

The crucifix inside the chapel.

the feet before dying away (one leg was subsequently cut off by a souvenir hunter). A plaque on the wall outside reads:

On est prié de respecter cette chapelle, où pendant la mémorable journée du 18 juin 1815 tant de vaillants défenseurs d'Hougoumont ont rendu le dernier soupir.

('Visitors are earnestly requested to tread this chapel with respect for within its walls on the memorable 18th June 1815 many of the brave defenders of Hougoumont passed to their rest.')

The chapel at Hougomont which miraculously survived the fire started by French howitzers.

A gate allows access from the building block into the walled garden to the east. Although the actual garden is now mere pastureland, you can still see some of the loopholes in the wall. In places the British guardsmen erected rough wooden platforms to enable them to fire over the wall. You will also find a monument here to the French soldiers who died attacking the farm, although very few of them actually managed to scale the wall into the garden.

The orchard further east changed hands several times during the battle, but is now an open field. Initially it was defended by the two light companies of the 1st Guards, until they were relieved early in the afternoon by the 3rd Guards under Major Francis Hepburn. Several units of German infantry also fought here.

Despite their incredible bravery and determination, the French never managed to capture the farm, for although they sometimes held the wood and orchard, they were unable to gain the most important parts, namely the garden and building block. The fighting here was probably the most intense of the entire battle and it lasted all day. 'No troops but the British could have held Hougoumont,' Wellington later remarked, 'and only the best of them at that.'

36

WELLINGTON'S CENTRE

From Hougoumont, follow the road back to the Lion Mound along the top of Wellington's ridge. This sector of the line bore the brunt of both the massed cavalry charges in the afternoon and the Imperial Guard attack in the evening.

To the north of the ridge are the reverse slopes where Wellington's battalions sheltered from the French artillery fire in the intervals between Napoleon's attacks. The troops would lie down in formation to escape the worst of the fire, while the soggy ground absorbed the impact of the projectiles and prevented many of them from ricocheting. Wellington's own batteries stood on the ridge crest, from where they could fire on the French formations attacking across the valley. Among them was 'G' Troop, Royal Horse Artillery and you will find a monument on the roadside marking its position. The battery had initially stood in reserve, but entered the front line here towards 5.00 pm, at the

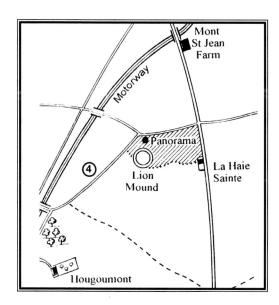

British Royal Horse Artillery galloping into action. *(ASKB)*

'Ah! that's the way I like to see horse-artillery move.'

height of the massed French cavalry charges. Wellington, on seeing the gun teams galloping up to their new position, exclaimed: 'Ah! that's the way I like to see horse-artillery move.' The battery commander, Captain Cavalié Mercer, vividly described in his journal how on coming up to the ridge crest, he was enveloped in

Monument marking the position of 'G' Troop, Royal Horse Artillery.

thick smoke and found that the air he was breathing was now suffocatingly hot, like that issuing from an oven. Through the smoke, Mercer saw French cavalry coming towards him at a brisk trot and immediately ordered his six guns to be unlimbered and formed up in a line ready for action. His postion was immediately behind the road that ran along the top of the ridge. As you can see, the ground on this side of the road is about two feet lower and this bank formed a natural rampart for Mercer's guns, as well as making their fire more murderous. He described how his battery repeatedly beat off the French horsemen:

Their pace was a slow but steady trot. None of your furious galloping charges was this, but a deliberate advance, at a deliberate pace, as of men resolved to carry their point. They moved in profound silence, and the only sound that could be heard from them amidst the incessant roar of battle was the low thunder-like reverberation of the ground beneath the simultaneous tread of so many horses.

Royal Horse Artillery gunners swinging a cannon into position.

Captain Mercer's guns halt the French Cuirassiers.

Mercer coolly held his fire until the leading ranks of horsemen were fifty or sixty yards away and then opened up with deadly effect:

> *Those who pushed forward over the heaps of carcasses of men and horses gained but a few paces in advance, there to fall in their turn and add to the difficulties of those succeeding them. The discharge of every gun was followed by a fall of men and horses like that of grass before the mower's scythe.*

By the end of the battle, a ghastly heap of mangled bodies lay in front of Mercer's battery, while his guns had recoiled back into a disordered line, his gunners being too exhausted to push them back into position after each shot.

A little further along the road is another memorial, to Lieutenant Augustin Demulder of the 5th Cuirassiers, one of the gallant French cavalrymen who were slain that day. Ironically, Demulder had been born in the Belgian town of Nivelles, just six miles from the battlefield on which he died.

This sector saw the last French attack when, in the evening, Napoleon sent in six battalions of his Imperial Guard. These crack troops advanced across the valley towards the area where the Lion Mound now stands. There were nearly 3000 of them and the

brunt of their assault fell on the British 1st Guards, who were lying down in line to shelter from French artillery fire. If you stand on the road immediately south of the Mound, you will be at the spot occupied by the 1st Guards, the point where the battle came to its epic climax. The action earned the regiment the proud title of the Grenadier Guards because at the time their Imperial Guard opponents were thought to be grenadiers. (They were probably, in fact, chasseurs, but wore very similar uniforms).

Wellington took personal command. When two battalions of the French guardsmen appeared on the ridge crest and were well within range, he ordered the 1st Guards to stand up and to fire a devastating volley of musketry. Captain Harry Weyland Powell described what happened next:

> *Whether it was from the sudden and unexpected appearance of a Corps so near them, which must have seemed as starting out of the ground, or the tremendously heavy fire we threw into them,* La Garde, *who had never before failed in an attack,* suddenly *stopped. Those who from a distance and more on the flank could see the affair, tell us that the effect*

The climax of the battle: Wellington orders the British 1st Guards to stand up, ready to meet the advance of the French Imperial Guard. (ASKB)

THE IMPERIAL GUARD ATTACK

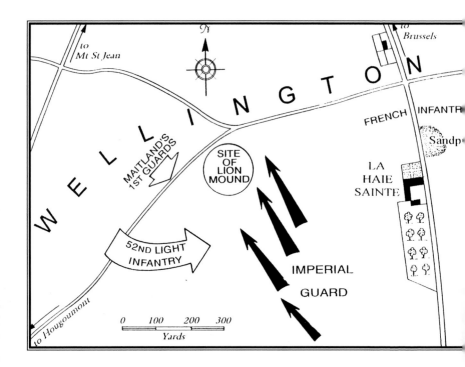

of our fire seemed to force the head of the Column bodily back.

The British charged and triumphantly chased the shattered guardsmen back down the forward slope of the ridge. But then another two Imperial Guard battalions came up and spearheaded a renewed advance, forcing the 1st Guards hurriedly to fall back to the ridge crest. Then, as the French marched up, something happened in Wellington's line further south. Lieutenant-Colonel Sir John Colborne boldly took his unit, the British 52nd Light Infantry, out of the front line and wheeled it round through ninety degrees to fire directly into the exposed left flank of the advancing Imperial Guardsmen. This decisive move, completed by a bayonet charge, overthrew the guardsmen and flung them back into the valley.

The French had staked everything on this attack and when they saw their supposedly invincible Guard falling back in defeat, they reacted with incredulous cries of *La garde recule!* 'The Guard is falling back!' Then spine-chilling shouts of 'we are betrayed' and 'everyone for himself' echoed around the battlefield as Napoleon's army disintegrated and began to run.

Lieutenant-Colonel Sir Augustus Frazer, commanding the Royal Horse Artillery, later wrote:

> *I have seen nothing like that moment, the sky literally darkened with smoke, the sun just going down, and which 'till then has not for some hours broken through the gloom of a dull day, the indescribable shouts of thousands where it was impossible to distinguish between friend and foe. Every man's arm seemed to be raised against that of every other. Suddenly, after the mingled mass had ebbed and flowed, the enemy began to yield; and cheerings and English huzzas announced that the day must be ours.*

Wellington triumphantly waved his hat three times to signal a general advance of his entire line forward into the valley to sweep the French from the field. Some of his officers urged him to be

Wellington waves his hat to signal a general advance of his army. (ASKB)

'Oh, damn it!
In for a penny,
in for a pound.'

cautious, but he would have none of it, exclaiming: 'Oh, damn it! In for a penny, in for a pound.' Then he galloped along his army to tell his troops: 'no cheering, my lads, but forward, and complete your victory.' The great battle was finally won.

Napoleon's Imperial Guard covers the rout of his army at the end of the battle. (ASKB)

THE PANORAMA

The white circular building at the foot of the Mound was erected between 1910 and 1912 and contains a spectacular panorama painting of the height of the massed French cavalry charges.

The brunt of these onslaughts hit Wellington's line between Hougoumont and La Haie Sainte. They began towards 4.00 pm when Marshal Ney saw some of Wellington's battalions retiring. In fact, they were merely moving back slightly to shelter on the reverse slopes of the ridge from the French gunfire, but the impetuous Ney mistakenly assumed that Wellington was retreating and promptly ordered the IV Cavalry Corps under General Edouard Milhaud to charge by bellowing the command: 'Forwards! The salvation of France is at stake!'

Milhaud's corps contained eight regiments of cuirassiers,

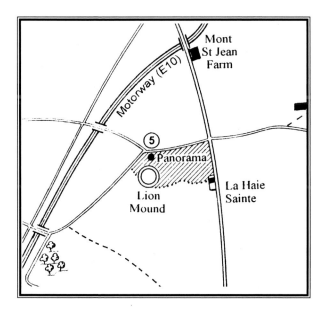

'Prepare to receive cavalry.'

French cuirassiers attacking a British square during the afternoon of the battle.

splendid heavy cavalrymen equipped with helmets and gleaming plates of armour to protect their chests and backs. As they moved off, they were followed by the élite light cavalry division of the Imperial Guard.

A young British officer, Ensign Rees Gronow of the 1st Guards, vividly remembered the first onset of the French cavalry:

> *Not a man present who survived could have forgotten in after life the awful grandeur of that charge. You perceived at a*

distance what appeared to be an overwhelming, long moving line, which, ever advancing, glittered like a stormy wave of the sea when it catches the sunlight.

Along Wellington's front line, the order rang out: 'Prepare to receive cavalry.' His infantry battalions promptly assumed hollow square formations – the standard defensive tactic for infantry beset by hostile cavalry. These squares had walls four men deep, bristled with bayonets all the way round and repeatedly blasted the horsemen with volleys of musketry. A typical square (or, more

Almost through – French cavalry struggle to break a square.

accurately, oblong) might contain five hundred men and have a frontage of about twenty-six yards and sides of around seven yards, although variations did exist. Because their horses refused to charge into what they saw as a solid object, the French cavalry did not charge headlong right on to the array of bayonets, but instead instinctively veered to either side and passed along the sides of the squares. Only a handful of daring individuals rode up and fired pistols into the squares, or hacked vainly at the bayonets with their swords.

The breastplates of the cuirassiers might deflect a sword slash or a musketball fired from a distance, but offered no protection against cannonballs or close-range musketry. Dismounted horsemen, weighed down by their armour and enormous boots, sprawled helplessly on the ground like so many overturned turtles, as Wellington laughingly recalled. Many promptly discarded their heavy armour before struggling to get away through the sticky mud.

In fact, it was extremely difficult for unsupported cavalry to break squares and Ney failed to back up his horsemen with infantry and artillery. Instead, his charges escalated during the afternoon as they sucked in the rest of Napoleon's reserve cavalry, namely the III Cavalry Corps of General François Kellermann and the heavy cavalry division of the Guard. An awesome array of 9000 horsemen now seethed and swarmed over the slippery slopes. They included lancers and green-coated dragoons, horse grenadiers in towering bearskins and armoured carabiniers and cuirassiers. Wellington's squares stood in a chequerboard pattern in order to create a deadly crossfire as the French cavalry thundered in like surf foaming around rocks on a beach. The scenes of chaos are vividly depicted in the panorama. Ensign Gronow remembered how:

Our square was a perfect hospital, being full of dead, dying, and mutilated soldiers. Inside we were nearly suffocated by the smoke and smell from burnt cartridges. It was impossible to move a yard without treading upon a wounded comrade, or upon the bodies of the dead; and the loud groans of the wounded and dying were most appalling.

Once the French had lost the impetus of a charge, Wellington's horsemen would counter-attack from reserve positions to the north and drive them off the ridge crest. In between each charge,

Centres of the squares became choked with British dead and wounded.

the French guns would open up again with murderous intensity from the other side of the valley. Wellington's own gunners would man their batteries on top of the ridge until the last moment and then, as the French thundered in once more, would either hide under their guns or dash for the safety of a nearby square.

The charges continued for over an hour-and-a-half until the French cavalry were exhausted. They had taken appalling casualties, with one regiment, the 6th Cuirassiers, losing a staggering eighty per cent of its officers. But despite this, and despite their failure to break through, they had attacked with such courage and determination that they won the admiration even of their foes.

The Panorama building, seen from the Lion Mound. Inside a spectacular mural depicts the massed French cavalry charges at the height of the battle.

LA HAIE SAINTE

You will now wish to see Wellington's other main strongpoint: the farm of La Haie Sainte in the centre of the battlefield. From the Lion Mound, go east along the ridge until you come to the crossroads. Cross over at the traffic lights and then follow the cycle track for three hundred yards along the eastern edge of the Brussels road until you see La Haie Sainte on the opposite side.

The farm has changed little over the years. It is smaller than Hougoumont, but still formidable since, as with most old Belgian farms, it was built around a courtyard to form a continuous defensive perimeter. The initial garrison was the green-coated 2nd Light battalion of the King's German Legion (KGL), a total of over 370 men commanded by Major George Baring. They were superb troops and carried the Baker rifle, which was accurate to 150 yards, about double

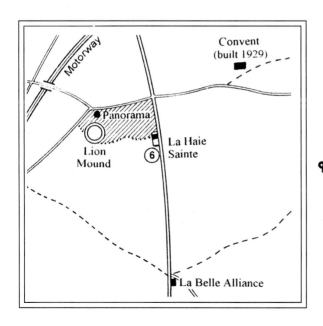

The Baker Rifle.

53

The farm of La Haie Sainte photographed some eighty years after the battle of Waterloo. A group of Victorian battlefield tourists can be seen passing the eastern gate.

The farm today with arrows indicating the direction of the French attack.

Barn

Main Gate

Farm House

Barricade

Original width of road

the range of the smooth-bore musket used by the vast majority of the infantry at Waterloo.

Baring had no entrenching tools or pioneers, but was able to knock three large loopholes in the wall on the eastern side of the farm and to barricade the Brussels road immediately outside. The situation was more serious on the western side of the courtyard, where the barn door had been burnt as firewood during the night since the men did not learn until the morning that the place would have to be defended. The open doorway was barricaded and would soon be further blocked by the bodies of seventeen Frenchmen.

The first French attack on La Haie Sainte came at 2.00 pm, as part of Napoleon's massive onslaught against Wellington's eastern wing. A brigade of infantry from the French I Corps was detached to assault the farm; Baring had to abandon the large orchard on the southern side, but held out inside the building block. The French abandoned the attack when British heavy cavalry smashed the rest of the I Corps in the open fields to the east.

Napoleon realised that La Haie Sainte held the key to victory. If he could capture the farm, he would be able to use it as an advanced base from which to pound Wellington's centre at dangerously close range. French infantry therefore renewed the

French troops, after overcoming the barricade, assault the main gateway on the eastern side of La Haie Sainte. (ASKB)

THE FALL OF LA HAIE SAINTE

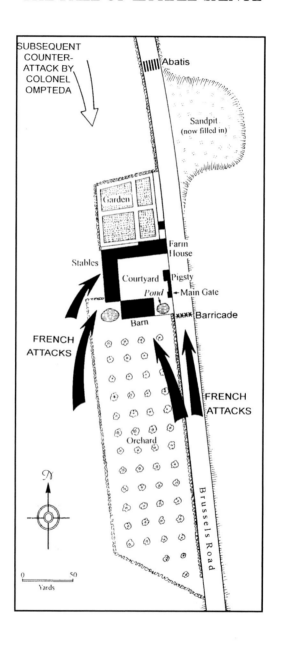

attack at 3.30 pm, but were again beaten off. Marshal Ney then began to lead masses of French cavalry past the farm to assail Wellington's infantry squares on the ridge to the north. Major Baring poured all the fire he could muster on to them as they rode past. Meanwhile, he also had to repel a series of French infantry attacks on the farm and as the afternoon wore on, he began to run dangerously low on rifle ammunition.

His pleas for more went unheeded and instead he merely received reinforcements: three more companies of KGL troops and about two hundred infantrymen from the Duchy of Nassau, one of the small German states to supply a contingent to Wellington's army. Fortunately, the Nassauers each carried a large cooking pot and when the barn roof caught fire, Baring was able to put it out by filling these pots with water from a pond in a

Major Baring, on horseback, directs the defence of La Haie Sainte shortly before its fall to the French. (ASKB)

'No man will desert you – we will fight and die with you.'

corner of the courtyard.

Towards 6.00 pm, the French attacked once again and now Baring was desperate. His men had practically run out of cartridges, but swore that 'no man will desert you – we will fight and die with you.' He recalled how:

> *Despising death, the French fought with a degree of courage which I had never before witnessed in Frenchmen. Favoured by their advancing in masses, every bullet of ours hit, and seldom were the effects limited to one assailant; this did not, however, prevent them from throwing themselves against the walls, and endeavouring to wrest the arms from the hands of my men, through the loopholes.*

French engineers smashed their way through the main gateway on the eastern face of the farm and fought hand-to-hand with the Germans. At the same time, infantrymen on the western side broke down a gate into the stables while some of their comrades clambered on to the roofs and fired down into the courtyard. Seeing that his position was untenable, Baring ordered his surviving soldiers to abandon the farm. One of them, Ensign George Frank, was wounded and unable to escape, so he hid under a bed in the farmhouse and remained there undiscovered, even though the French murdered two of his injured comrades lying in the same room.

The fall of La Haie Sainte had an immediate impact on the battle. Hitherto, it had been a thorn in the side of the French during their attacks on the ridge to the north. But they now brought guns and troops up to the farm and opened fire on Wellington's front line at close range. A most critical onslaught developed which, though ultimately beaten off, dangerously wore down Wellington's line.

It was during these tense moments that one of Wellington's brigade commanders, Colonel Christian von Ompteda, was ordered to lead a desperate counter-attack from the ridge crest towards the garden of La Haie Sainte. He protested that such a move would be suicidal in the presence of nearby French cavalry, but was overruled by the young and headstrong Prince of Orange, who commanded the centre of Wellington's army. French horsemen duly cut the 5th Line battalion, KGL to pieces and Ompteda himself was tragically shot dead near the northern face of the farm.

La Haie Sainte remained in French hands until Napoleon's

Re-enactors uniformed as the 2nd Light battalion KGL

A memorial plaque on the wall of La Haie Sainte.

TO MAJ. BARING AND THE 2nd LIGHT
Btn KGL's HEROIC DEFENCE OF
LA HAIE SAINTE 18 JUNE 1815
ALSO TO COL. von OMPTEDA WHO FELL
LEADING A BRAVE COUNTER-ATTACK
AFTER THE FALL OF THE FARM

DEDICATED BY
BEXHILL-ON-SEA ENGLAND
A KING'S GERMAN LEGION
GARRISON 1804-14

IM GEDENKEN AN DIE HELDENHAFTE VERTEIDIGUNG
VON LA HAIE SAINTE AM 18. JUNI 1815 DURCH
MAJOR BARING MIT DEM 2. LEICHTEN BATL.
DER KGL. DEUTSCHEN LEGION UND
AN OBERST von OMPTEDA, DER BEIM TAPFEREN
GEGENANGRIFF FIEL NACH DEM VERLUST DER FARM.

army broke and fled at the end of the battle. Today, plaques on the walls of the farm pay tribute to the bravery of both sides. One of them was placed there by the inhabitants of Bexhill-on-sea, a coastal resort in southern England where the KGL was stationed early in the Napoleonic wars when it was feared that the French might try to invade.

As you return from La Haie Sainte to the crossroads, you pass two monuments. On the western side of the Brussels road is a column to the memory of one of Wellington's ADCs, Lieutenant-Colonel the Hon. Sir Alexander Gordon, who was mortally wounded. Steps lead up to the column, which is sited on top of a bank that marks the original level of the ground in this sector before the soil nearby was removed to form the Lion Mound. Opposite is the Hanoverian Monument, dedicated to those of the King's German Legion who fell in the battle.

View from the Hanoverian monument, looking south along the Brussels road, La Haie Sainte is on the right.

WELLINGTON'S EASTERN WING

Whent you reach the crossroads, examine the nearby cluster of monuments. One of them commemorates Wellington's Belgian troops, and another is to Lieutenant-General Sir Thomas Picton, a fiery Welshman who commanded the sector east of the crossroads where Napoleon attacked in the afternoon.

To examine Picton's position, move eastwards along the cobbled road that follows the ridge for seven hundred yards. At the time of the battle, this road was a dirt track bordered on either side by a broken hedge. Immediately behind it stood two-and-a-half batteries of artillery and a brigade of Dutch-Belgian infantry, supported a hundred yards to the north by two British infantry brigades on more sheltered reverse slopes. A quarter of-

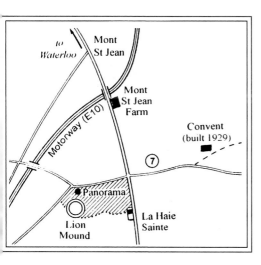

Monument to the Belgians killed on 18 June 'fighting for the defence of the flag and the honour of arms.'

La Haie Sainte

FRENCH INFANTRY COLUMN

a-mile further to the rear were some of Wellington's cavalry in reserve. Out in front, meanwhile, a screen of skirmishers extended all along the forward slopes of the ridge and an avanced post of the British 95th Rifles occupied a sandpit next to the Brussels road. (This pit was filled in after the battle, apparently being used as a mass grave, but used to be where the Hanoverian monument now stands).

If you stand on the cobbled road, face south and look towards the shallow ridge on the French side of the valley, three-quarters-of-a-mile away. Napoleon assembled at least fifty-four guns along the front of his eastern wing in a massed battery that exploded into action early in the afternoon. 'One could almost feel the undulation of the air from the multitude of cannon-shot,' wrote one British subaltern. Fortunately for the British, the previous night's rain had softened the ground, which muffled the shells' bursts and absorbed the inpact of many of the cannonballs. Most of Wellington's troops were hidden, and to some extent protected by the ridge, while the clouds of smoke soon forced the French gunners to fire blind.

This bombardment was merely the curtain-raiser and at 2.00 pm, there came the actual assault by the 16,000 infantry of the French I Corps. To cover the flank of the attack, a brigade of cuirassiers rode forward on the western side of the Brussels road, while an infantry brigade assaulted the farm of La Haie Sainte in the first, vain, attempt to capture it. East of the farm, the remaining infantry marched across the valley in four massive columns, each of them 180 men wide and up to twenty-four ranks deep. Wellington's guns did fearsome damage by sending

Lion Mound   Crossroads   Brussels Road

FRENCH INFANTRY COLUMN

Picton's Infantry

Royal Dragoons

Picton's Infantry

Hedgerow   Hedgerow

Picton's sector of the ridge, looking west to the farm of La Haie Sainte and the Lion Mound. Picton's infantry were ranged in two ranks and consequently were able to bring to bear every musket against the packed ranks of French infantry.

cannonballs tearing right through the dense formations.

The French columns were staggered, so that they reached the ridge crest in succession from west to east and in fact the fourth, easternmost, column never had time to arrive at all. At first, the action swung in favour of the French for they evicted the 95th Rifles from the sandpit and broke the Dutch-Belgian infantry brigade along the ridge crest, causing most of it to fall back in disorder. But then Picton's battalions waiting in the second line advanced from the reverse slopes and counter-attacked to the wailing of bagpipes from the Black Watch, Cameron and Gordon Highlanders.

Picton had only about 3000 infantry to oppose the French, but his battalions were formed into lines just two ranks deep, which enabled every man to fire his musket. In contrast, only the front three ranks of each French column could fire without hitting their comrades in front and although the first two columns halted in

Lieutenant-General Sir Thomas Picton. A rough and foul-mouthed man, Picton was nonetheless a great leader and was shot dead while heroically cheering on his men. He wore civilian clothes rather than a uniform, including a shabby greatcoat and top hat, and carried an umbrella. (ASKB)

front of the road on which you are standing and tried to deploy, they merely fell into greater confusion. For a while the outcome of this infantry clash teetered in the balance. Wellington himself intervened to rally some Highlanders, while Picton toppled from his horse after being shot dead as he cheered his men on: 'Charge! Hurrah! Hurrah!'

The westernmost French column was finally overthrown after one of its officers was shot dead as he tried to seize the Regimental Colour of the British 32nd Foot. But the second column was still trading fire and the third, apparently not stopping to deploy, had pushed right on to the ridge crest and was fiercely engaged with the 92nd (Gordon) Highlanders. Then, suddenly, the British Union Brigade of 900 heavy cavalrymen burst decisively into the fray. (At the same time, the Household Brigade, consisting of the 1st and 2nd Life Guards, the 1st Dragoon Guards and the Royal Horse Guards, routed the French cavalry west of the Brussels road). The Union Brigade, which had advanced from its reserve position to the north before being unleashed, had been hidden by the ridge until it was right on top

Picton's monument.

CHARGE OF THE BRITISH HEAVY CAVALRY

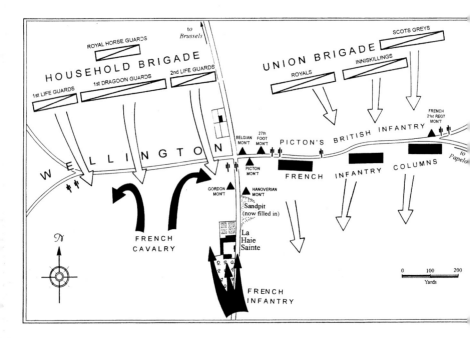

of the astounded French infantry. It consisted of three magnificent regiments: the English Royal Dragoons, the Irish Inniskilling Dragoons and the Scots Greys, which ferociously cut their way into the now disordered French infantry. Some Frenchmen fought like tigers, but most were so jammed together that they were powerless to defend themselves. Disordered masses of men threw down their muskets and poured back across the valley.

The most famous incident during these moments was the charge of the Scots Greys at the eastern end of Picton's line. You will find a monument here to the 21st Line infantry, which as part of the third French column came up to the ridge crest at this point. Then the Scots Greys, yelling 'Scotland for ever!', appeared

66

'Scotland for ever!'

The Scots Greys and Gordon Highlanders charge the French.

The Scots Greys seize the eagle standard of the French 45th Line infantry.
(ASKB)

over the ridge, charged through the ranks of the 92nd Highlanders and fell on the French. The two Scottish regiments cheered each other on as if they were half-mad, with the 92nd sallying forth in the wake of the Greys to gather up scores of prisoners.

A British infantry officer later wrote:

I remember a dreadful confusion, thick smoke, horses and men tumbling headlong; soldiers receiving their death wounds, springing up and falling down dead! ...Then a great body of French soldiers in disorder, throwing

Sergeant Ewart fights his way back with his trophy – the standard of the 45th.

69

Corporal Stiles of the Royal Dragoons brandishes his trophy, the eagle of the 105th Line.

> *down their arms and accoutrements, and calling out "Prisonniers! prisonniers!" driven on by the cavalry, coming towards us. The solid mass [of French infantry] I had seen twenty minutes before was there no more, and had now become a defenceless crowd.*

Amidst the indescribable chaos, Captain Alexander Kennedy

Clark and Corporal Francis Stiles of the Royal Dragoons seized the precious eagle standard of the French 105th Line, while Sergeant Charles Ewart of the Greys captured that of the 45th Line; these were the only eagles to be captured in the battle. Over two thousand prisoners were also taken and an onlooker likened the British horsemen to a cloud of locusts laying waste to everything. But, elated by their success, the dragoons lost control and charged too far, on to the far side of the valley. Here at last they tried to rally but, disorganised and with their horses blown, they were now terribly vulnerable and in no state to resist a devastating counter-attack by fresh cavalry from Napoleon's reserves. Many isolated dragoons, including the Union Brigade commander, Major-General the Hon. Sir William Ponsonby, were mercilessly speared by French lancers. Although the survivors gradually trickled back to their lines, they were practically a spent force for the rest of the day. Wellington had beaten off an extremely serious attack, but at a heavy price.

The French subsequently concentrated their efforts against the centre, between Hougoumont and La Haie Sainte, so this eastern sector of Wellington's front never saw another major assault, although heavy skirmishing and minor attacks continued here into the evening. Lieutenant Johnny Kincaid of the 95th Rifles, who fought in this part of the line, wrote:

For the next two or three succeeding hours there was no

A memorial to the French 21st Line infantry, erected where the regiment attacked Wellington's eastern wing.

Monument to the 27th (or the Inniskilling) Regiment of Foot.

variety with us, but one continued blaze of musketry. The smoke hung so thick about, that, although not more than eighty yards asunder, we could only distinguish each other by the flashes of the pieces.

One of the monuments near the crossroads commemorates the heroism of the 27th Foot. This infantry unit originally stood in reserve, but moved into the front line after the charge of the Union Brigade. Standing on an exposed mound immediately north-east of the crossroads, it lost sixty-six per cent of its men, including eleven of its twelve most senior officers. Lieutenant Kincaid described the unit after the battle as 'lying literally dead, in square, a few yards behind us.'

PAPELOTTE FARM

C ontinue eastwards and visit Wellington's far left flank. The cobbled road that has hitherto run along the ridge crest veers off to the south-east and leads you down the forward slopes to the farm of Papelotte, one of Wellington's four strongpoints at this end of the line. The other three stand a few hundred yards further east: the farm of La Haye, the village of Smohain and the château of Frischermont.

As soon as you see the difficult terrain in this area, including the brook and the sunken lanes, you will understand why the French did not launch serious attacks or an outflanking move here. Wellington was able to hold the four strongpoints with just one brigade of Nassau infantry, a total of 3000 men under Prince Bernhard of Saxe-Weimar. In support on the ridge crest to the north stood some Hanoverian infantry and two brigades of British

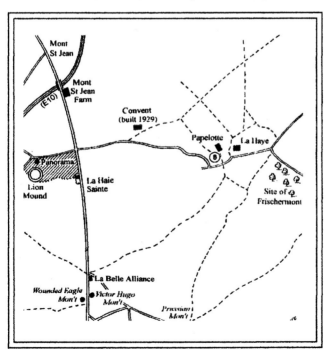

Papelotte as it appeared in the nineteenth century and as it appears today (right).

light cavalry under Major-Generals Sir John Vandeleur and Sir Hussey Vivian; these supporting troops were transferred in the evening to shore up Wellington's centre.

French infantry first attacked Prince Bernhard's Nassauers in the early afternoon and periodically renewed their assaults for the rest of the day. Most of the fighting was mere skirmishing, but some of the buildings occasionally changed hands. Be aware that the village of Smohain is now called La Marache; it has not

Papelotte (on the right), seen from the French side of the valley.

expanded significantly, although its old houses have been replaced by more modern ones.

The château of Frischermont was demolished in 1857, while Papelotte was rebuilt after being devastated by fire during the battle, with a belvedere over its main gateway being added in 1860. The farm of La Haye has also been rebuilt: in 1815 its buildings were only one storey high and had roofs of thatch and walls of cob, a composition of clay, gravel and straw.

The Nassauers came under increasing pressure as the day wore on and at 7.30 pm were on the point of giving way when the

head of the Prussian I Corps under General Hans von Ziethen arrived in the nick of time from the north-east. Other Prussian units had already been in action for three hours further south around the village of Plancenoit, but now Wellington's left flank was about to receive direct support.

Initially, however, a tragic incident of friendly fire occurred as the Nassauers, forced out of Smohain, retreated towards Ziethen's Prussians who, in the confusion of battle, mistook them for the French and opened fire. This proved a temporary setback and the Prussian artillery helped check the French. Ziethen then thrust south-westwards, through Smohain and diagonally across the battlefield into Napoleon's positions, thereby helping to precipitate the rout of his army soon after 8.00 pm. One of Ziethen's men, Henri Nieman of the 6th Uhlans, described how:

At about nine o'clock in the evening the battlefield was almost cleared of the French army. It was an evening no pen is able to picture: the surrounding villages yet in flames, the lamentations of the wounded of both armies, the singing for joy; no one is able to describe nor find a name to give to those horrible scenes.

You will probably want to collect your car at the Lion Mound in order to drive to the French side of the valley. But if you have enough time and energy, you can walk there instead, from Papelotte along the dirt track that leads to La Belle Alliance. It was along this track that the French I Corps formed up at the start of the battle and from where it attacked across the valley at 2.00 pm towards Point Seven following the preliminary bombardment by the Great Battery. The battery's guns were lined up immediately north of the track and you can see their field of fire and how most of Wellington's troops would have been hidden behind the opposite ridge.

LA BELLE ALLIANCE

To drive from the Lion Mound to the French side of the valley, simply go east to the crossroads and then turn right on to the Brussels road. On the horizon you will see the inn of La Belle Alliance, which stood at the centre of Napoleon's front line at the start of the battle. Towards 10.00 am, his units took up their positions in a magnificent parade that intimidated many of Wellington's troops. The sound of bands drifted across the valley and as Napoleon himself recalled: *'La terre paraissait orgueilleuse de porter tant de braves.'* ('The earth seemed proud to bear so many brave men.')

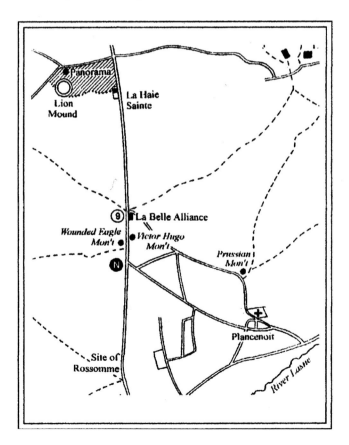

(a)

La Belle Alliance: (a) During the battle.
(b) In the 1820s. *(ASKB)*
(c) In the 1890s and catering for the battlefield tourists.
(d) In 1998.

(b)

(c)

(d)

'The earth seemed proud to bear so many brave men.'

On the morning of the battle Napoleon receives a salute from his men. (ASKB)

One of his soldiers vividly describes the scene:

L'empereur passa alors devant le front de tous les corps, et, par un mouvement spontané qui ressemblait à une commotion électrique, casques, shakos, bonnets à poil furent agités au bout des sabres ou des baïonnettes aux cris frénétiques de Vive l'empereur!

('Then the emperor passed in front of all the corps. With a spontaneous movement which resembled an electric current, helmets, shakos and bearskins were waved on the tips of sabres or bayonets to frenzied cheering of "Long live the Emperor!"')

On either side of La Belle Alliance stood a corps: II Corps to the west and I Corps to the east, with massed cavalry waiting in

80

support four hundred yards to the rear. Finally, in the centre and drawn up along the Brussels road south of La Belle Alliance, were the reserves: the VI Corps and the infantry and artillery units of the Imperial Guard.

Although La Belle Alliance served as a field hospital, there was little fighting nearby because for most of the battle the French were attacking Wellington's army on the other side of the valley. Napoleon left Marshal Ney, his chief subordinate, to lead the attacks, while he himself exercised a more general command from the rear.

Two mounds on the western edge of the Brussels road served as his main command posts, but offered limited views. One of them was immediately south of the so-called Wounded Eagle monument and the other, on which he spent most of the day, was 1200 yards further south near the farm of Rossomme, which burnt down in 1895. A French general watched from afar:

> *Je l'ai vu, avec ma lunette, se promener de long en large, revêtu de sa redingote grise, et s'accouder souvent sur la petite table qui porte sa carte.*

('I saw him, with my telescope, walking up and down, dressed in his grey greatcoat, and often leaning on the small table bearing his maps.')

Another French officer was able to watch Napoleon at closer quarters, from the foot of the mound near Rossomme:

> *Assis sur une chaise de paille, devant une grossière table de ferme, il y tenait sa carte ouverte, sa fameuse lorgnette à la main était souvent braquée sur les divers points de la bataille, au repos de son oeil, il ramassait des pailles de blé, qu'il*

Napoleon, in his famous grey overcoat, considers the situation whilst his officers await his orders.

French infantry on the march. (ASKB)

portait à sa bouche comme curedent; placé à sa gauche, le maréchal Soult [son major-général], seul, attendait ses ordres, et dix pas en arrière était groupé tout son état-major à cheval. Pour arriver à l'Empereur avec plus de facilité, des sapeurs du génie traçaient des rampes sur le pourtour du mamelon. Jamais on ne rencontrera un calme plus grand, plus parfait que celui de Napoleon, le jour de cette bataille... On voyait la satisfaction peinte dans ses traits, tout allait bien, et nul doute qu'à ce moment, il ne crut sa bataille gagnée. Je l'admirai longtemps, mes yeux ne pouvaient le quitter, c'était le génie de la guerre. Je partis enfin... et ne le revis plus; j'ai ce dernier souvenir toujours présent.

('Seated on a straw chair, in front of a coarse farm table, he was holding his map open on the table. His famous spyglass in his hand was often trained on the various points of the battle. When resting his eye, he used to pick up straws of wheat which he carried in his mouth as a toothpick. Stationed on his left, Marshal Soult [his chief-of-staff] alone waited for his orders and ten paces to the rear were grouped all his staff on horseback. Sappers of the engineers were opening ramps around the mound so that people could reach the Emperor more easily. Never will

Marshal Soult, Napoleon's chief-of-staff. He wasn't as confident of victory as his master for he had fought against Wellington in the Peninsula.

The routed French army after Waterloo.

one meet a greater or more perfect calm than that of Napoleon on the day of this battle... Satisfaction could be seen written on his face and there is no doubt that at this moment he thought his battle was won. I admired him for a long time, my eyes were unable to leave him. He was the genius of war. I left at last... and I never saw him again. I have this ever-present last memory.')

You will also see the bank off the road between La Belle Alliance and Plancenoit signposted as Napoleon's observation post, but he was rarely, if ever, there.

One reason why Napoleon lost the battle was that he was too far to the rear and too distracted by the Prussians on his eastern flank. From this position he could not properly supervise the headstrong Ney and prevent him from launching the massive, unsupported charges of the French cavalry. Only in the evening did he ride forward into the valley, to a point south of La Haie Sainte, to watch his Imperial Guard attack Wellington's ridge.

It was after the repulse of the Guard that the fighting finally shifted to the French side of the valley. As the victorious allies swept across the battlefield, it was the Guard, some of whose

Napoleon sheltering in a square of his Imperial Guard before leaving the battlefield. (ASKB)

Napoleon leaves the battlefield, having suffered his final defeat. (ASKB)

After the battle: Imperial Guardsmen lying dead on the moonlit battlefield. (ASKB)

General Pierre Cambronne, commander of the 1st Chasseurs of the Imperial Guard. (ASKB)

battalions had been held back in reserve, that tried to cover the rout of Napoleon's army. Two hundred and fifty yards south of La Belle Alliance, you will see a monument on the western edge of the Brussels road adorned with the statue of a wounded eagle in bronze and inscribed: *Aux derniers combattants de la Grande Armée* (To the last combatants of the Grand Army). The eagle was the symbol of Napoleon's empire and the monument recalls the desperate defiance of the Guard in the dying moments of the battle. Though fatally injured and with one of its wings shot through with musketry, the eagle still grasps a standard with one claw and threatens the enemy with the other.

Over the years, a legend has emerged of the Guard standing to the last man. But like all such heroic episodes, from the defence of Masada against the Romans in 73 AD to the siege of the Alamo by the Mexicans in

1836, the final moments of Waterloo are a mixture of truth, myth and outright fabrication. One version, popularised by the great French writer, Victor Hugo (1802–85), has a British officer invite the guardsmen to surrender, to be answered by General Pierre Cambronne with the expletive, *Merde!* The British then respond with a thunderous volley of artillery that annihilates the French. Another, less likely, version records Cambronne's answer as, *la Garde meurt et ne se rend pas*: 'the Guard dies and does not surrender.'

The reality was more complicated. The Guard certainly suffered heavy casualties, but instead of standing to the last man, it mostly disintegrated into small groups conducting a fighting retreat from the battlefield. Cambronne himself was wounded and captured. The most spectacular defiance came from the 2nd Battalion, 3rd Grenadiers. Decimated by fire at close-range, the unit retreated in a hollow square formation through the open fields north-west of the Wounded Eagle. After taking increasingly heavy casualties, it collapsed into a triangle, then fired a final volley, cheered 'Long live the Emperor!' and broke up.

You will have noticed a tall column on the eastern side of the road, about one hundred yards north of the Wounded Eagle. This commemorates Victor Hugo,

Detail of the Victor Hugo monument.

The Wounded Eagle monument.

Wellington and Blücher meet near La Belle Alliance at the end of the battle.
(ASKB)

who visited the battlefield while writing *Les Misérables*, first published in 1862 and now a hit musical. He vividly described Waterloo in the novel, but explained away Napoleon's defeat as the result of a sunken lane into which the massed French cavalry charges supposedly foundered – a myth that endures to this day.

Work began on the Victor Hugo monument in 1912, but was interrupted by two world wars and a lack of funds and has never been fully completed. The Gallic cock originally intended for the summit has never been put in place and the column attained its present state only in 1956. It bears a large bronze medallion of Hugo and several lines from one of his poems about the 'mournful plain' of Waterloo.

It was near La Belle Alliance that Wellington and Blücher met by chance after driving the French from the field. It was 9.00 pm and dusk had fallen. *Mein lieber Kamerad!* exclaimed the exuberant Blücher. *Quelle affaire!* ('My dear comrade! What a to-do!') The British call the battle 'Waterloo', after the village where Wellington had his headquarters, but the Prussians called it 'La Belle Alliance', which by coincidence was French for 'the fine alliance.'

Napoleon, meanwhile, had ridden off the battlefield in the midst of his routed army and was destined to spend the last six years of his life in exile, brooding on his downfall. 'Death is nothing,' he remarked, 'but to live defeated is to die a thousand times every day.'

PLANCENOIT

Y ou will now want to see the south-eastern corner of the battlefield, where the Prussians were engaged, so leave the Brussels road at La Belle Alliance and follow the signposts to the village of Plancenoit. On the way, you will pass a memorial to the 5th Cuirassiers, one of the French cavalry regiments that repeatedly charged Wellington's squares during the afternoon. The unit was deployed nearby at the start of the battle.

Plancenoit is a quiet village and usually has plenty of room for parking. Ferocious fighting raged here during the late afternoon and evening as the Prussians attacked Napoleon's right wing. It is still possible to follow the action here, even though the village has grown considerably in size. It had only 520 inhabitants at the time of the battle.

Wellington expected his Prussian allies to join him sooner than they in fact did. But to reach the battlefield, they had to march

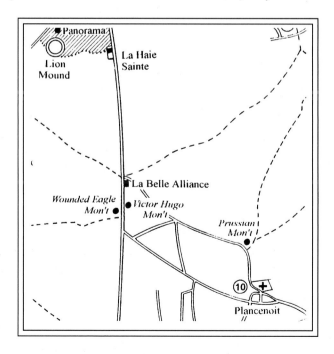

THE PRUSSIAN MARCH TO WATERLOO

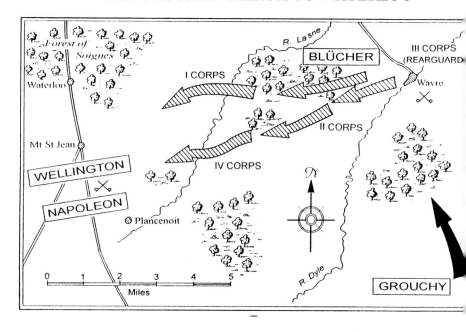

Blücher exhorts his Prussians on the march to the battlefield. (ASKB)

from Wavre, almost ten miles to the east. One corps remained there as a rearguard, while the other three set off in succession throughout the morning and early afternoon. They had to cross difficult, muddy terrain using poor quality tracks in the absence of any paved roads. But Blücher was everywhere, urging his men on.

The Prussian commander, Field Marshal Gebhard Leberecht von Blücher. His determination to join Wellington at Waterloo was the key to victory. (ASKB)

We must get on! I have given my word to Wellington, and you will surely not make me break it. Only exert yourselves a few hours longer, children, and certain victory is ours.

By 4.30 pm, Blücher had arrived on the eastern edge of the battlefield with his leading units, part of the IV Corps under General Friedrich Wilhelm von Bülow. Wellington was now under such heavy attack that Blücher and his subordinates saw that they had to make an immediate diversion, even though they did not have all their forces in hand. They therefore advanced out of the cover of the woods with what troops they had and opened fire with artillery to signal their entry into the battle.

Napoleon had discovered three hours earlier that the Prussians were approaching and had been forced to detach 8000 men from his reserves to protect his exposed eastern flank. These troops, the VI Corps under General Georges Mouton, the Count of Lobau and two light cavalry divisions, had taken up a position at right angles to Napoleon's front line and now tried to contain the Prussians. Already, therefore, the Prussian intervention had diverted crucial French manpower and prevented it from being used against Wellington.

The Prussian 2nd Infantry attacking the 1st Battalion, 2nd Chasseurs of the Old Guard in the Village of Plancenoit. Note the church on fire in the background. (ASKB)

So far, the Prussians had only 16,000 men on the battlefield, but would be continually reinforced until at the end of the day they would have some 40,000 in action. Gradually pushing back the outnumbered Lobau, they linked up with Wellington's far eastern flank at Frischermont in the north and filled the open countryside further south. They covered a front of one-and-a-quarter miles, but made their main thrust in the south, in a bid to cut the Brussels road – Napoleon's line of retreat – and hence trap and destroy his army. Before they could reach the road, they had to take the low-lying village of Plancenoit, which lay 1000 yards east of it, and this was why Plancenoit became crucially important to both sides. *Wenn wir nur das verfluchte Dorf hätten.* ('If only we had the damned village!') Blücher exclaimed.

Towards 6.00 pm, the Prussians managed to seize most of Plancenoit after pounding it with six batteries of artillery. Napoleon had to commit 4000 infantrymen of the Imperial Guard – the Young Guard division under General Philibert Duhesme – in order to regain the village. Two subsequent Prussian assaults failed with heavy losses, but the third proved a success and forced Napoleon to intervene yet again. This time he sent two Old Guard battalions, about 1000 men in all, which quickly stormed the village at the bayonet and swept out the Prussians.

By now it was 7.30 pm and Napoleon had temporarily contained the Prussians using the Guard inside Plancenoit and Lobau's VI

Corps to the north. He took advantage of the lull to send some of his remaining Guard battalions against Wellington's army in a final, doomed attempt to break through. But then a fresh Prussian infantry brigade, the head of the II Corps under General Georg von Pirch I, arrived and

Street fighting in Plancenoit.

spearheaded a renewed assault on Plancenoit involving 20,000 troops. Bitter hand-to-hand fighting raged in the streets, orchards and gardens, but the 5000 defenders were forced to give way when they saw Prussian forces outflanking the village to the south and threatening to cut them off. The triumphant Prussians had broken through at last, but as they poured westwards to the

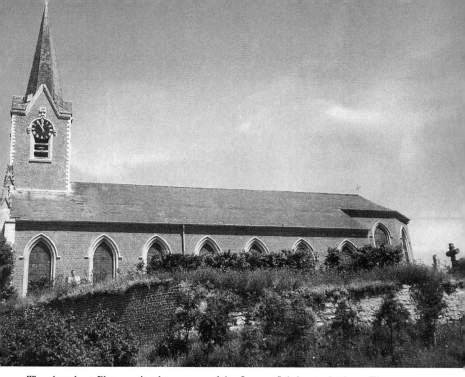

The church at Plancenoit where some of the fiercest fighting took place. The churchyard walls were used by the French to pour fire down on the Prussians.

Brussels road they found that Napoleon's army had already disintegrated and was fleeing southwards – they were too late to block its line of retreat. Despite this, some of their less exhausted units set off in pursuit and harried the panic-stricken fugitives into the night.

You should first drive to the centre of Plancenoit to see the Church of St Catherine, where some of the fiercest fighting raged. The church, which was set on fire during the battle, was rebuilt in 1857. The French used its walled churchyard to pour fire down on to Prussian units that were trying to force their way along the roads on either side. Note that the churchyard in 1815 was more closely surrounded by houses. General Jean Pelet, who defended it with the 1st battalion, 2nd Chasseurs of the Old Guard, described the murderous action:

> *Je me maintenais au milieu de cette grêle d'obus, du feu qui commençait à s'allumer dans diverses maisons, d'une fusillade terrible et continuelle; ils nous environnaient d'une multitude de tirailleurs. N'importe, je tenais comme un démon, je ne pouvais plus réunir mes hommes, mais ils étaient tous nichés, et faisaient sur l'ennemi un feu meurtrier.*

95

Prussian memorial at Plancenoit at the end of the nineteenth century.

('I persisted in the midst of a hail of howitzer shells, in the midst of fires which were beginning to flare up in various houses and in the midst of a terrible, continuous musketry. I held on like a demon; I could not gather my men but they were all under cover and were pouring on the enemy a murderous fire.')

Inside the church, you will find a tablet dedicated to a young French artillery officer who died in the battle, while on the wall outside the entrance door are a couple of memorial plaques. In the northern outskirts of the village is a monument to the Young Guard, whose commander, General Duhesme, was mortally wounded in the head by a shell burst. Nearby stands the Prussian memorial, erected on a mound once occupied by a French battery and inscribed in German: *Die gefallenen Helden ehrt dankbar König und Vaterland. Sie ruhn in Frieden.*

('To the dead heroes, their grateful King and Country. May they rest in peace').

NAPOLEON'S HEADQUARTERS

To end your tour, return to the N5 (the Brussels road) and drive southwards until you see signs for Le Caillou, the farm that served as Napoleon's quarters on the night before the battle. It was here that he held his pre-battle conference with his senior generals at 8.00 am on the morning of the battle. Some of his subordinates, who unlike him had experience of fighting Wellington and the British in previous years, lacked his confidence in an easy victory. He dismissed their fears, telling them that Wellington was a bad general and the

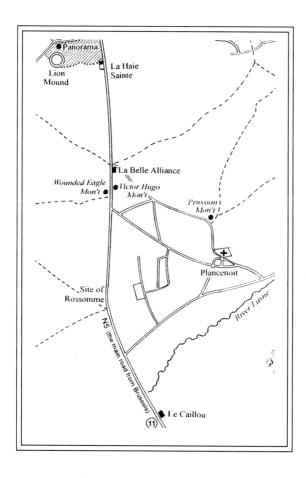

Le Caillou today.

Napoleon confers on the morning of Waterloo with General François Haxo, the commander of the Imperial Guard Engineeers. (ASKB)

British bad troops. *Messieurs, si mes ordres sont bien exécutés, nous coucherons à Bruxelles.* ('Gentlemen,' he assured them, 'if my orders are carried out well, we will sleep at Brussels.') He then left to inspect the battlefield and review his army before starting the battle.

Napoleon was one of the greatest commanders of history, but went down to defeat at Waterloo mainly because he seriously under-estimated his enemy. Even so, it was a near run thing. 'I never took so much trouble about any battle,' Wellington wrote,

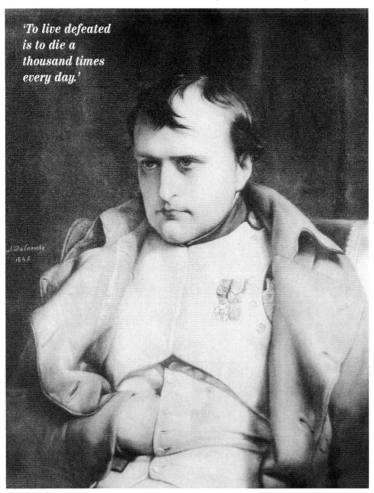

'To live defeated is to die a thousand times every day.'

Napoleon faces defeat. (ASKB)

and 'never was so near being beat.'

Le Caillou was destroyed by fire the day after the battle, but later rebuilt. It now contains a museum dedicated to the French Emperor's glory, although the authenticity of some of the furniture on display is suspect. One of the more unusual exhibits is a skeleton of a soldier, together with the uniform buttons that made possible his identification as a French hussar. He was clearly hit in the head by a ball and from the gash in his skull seems to have received a sabre cut.

In the walled orchard next to Le Caillou is a monument to the 1st Battalion, 1st Chasseurs of the Old Guard and on it are inscribed the names of the famous battle honours that the unit won under Napoleon. The battalion guarded his quarters and baggage and escorted him from the battlefield at the end of the day. In the adjacent garden is a little ossuary, erected in 1912 to hold some of the bones found on the battlefield.

Monument in the orchard of Le Caillou, where the 1st Battalion, 1st Chasseurs of the Old Guard bivouacked the night before the battle.

THE CASUALTIES

Before you leave, spare a thought for the victims of the epic clash. Wellington lost 15,000 men killed, wounded and missing – about twenty-two per cent of his force. Blücher lost 7000 of his Prussians and Napoleon about 30,000 men, plus several thousand more prisoners or deserters. As a British officer later wrote: 'This was the last, the greatest, and the most uncomfortable heap of glory that I ever had a hand in. After most battles,' he added, 'officers would visit neighbouring units to ask, "who's hit?" After Waterloo they inquired, "who's alive?"'

Another British veteran wrote:

I had been over many a field of battle, but with the exception of one spot at New Orleans, and the breach of Badajos, I had never seen anything to be compared with what I saw. At Waterloo the whole field from right to left was a mass of dead bodies. In one spot, to the right of La Haye Sainte, the French Cuirassiers were literally piled on each other; many soldiers not wounded lying under their horses; others, fearfully

The carnage-strewn battlefield on the following morning. (ASKB)

wounded, occasionally with their horses struggling upon their
wounded bodies. The sight was sickening, and I had no means
or power to assist them.

Waterloo has no cemetery. Except for a few officers, the dead were either burned or buried in unmarked mass graves. Bones uncovered in the years immediately after the battle were often taken by souvenir hunters, or ground into fertiliser for use on farmers' fields.

Even with the help of local people, it took several days to remove the wounded from the battlefield. Practically all the buildings in the neighbourhood, including the churches, served as makeshift hospitals. But most of the injured were taken further back, to Brussels or other towns and cities such as Antwerp, Ghent, Bruges, Ostend, Namur, Louvain, Liège and Maastricht in order to relieve the pressure on facilities.

The most important of Wellington's field hospitals was the farm of Mont St Jean, conveniently situated alongside the paved Brussels road six hundred yards north of his front line. A plaque commemorates the surgeons stationed here and was erected in 1981 by the Royal Army Medical Corps. One of the most famous casualties to receive treatment at the farm was Lieutenant-Colonel Lord Fitzroy Somerset, Wellington's Military Secretary, who had his arm amputated and, as Field Marshal Lord Raglan, later commanded the British army in the Crimean war from 1854 until his death the following year. The Prince of Orange also received first aid at the farm after being wounded in the shoulder.

Assistant-Surgeon William Gibney of the 15th Hussars described the horrific scenes that occurred on the road running past the farm:

Nothing could exceed the misery exhibited on this road,
which, being the highpave, or I might say the stone causeway
leading to Brussels, was crowded to excess with our wounded
and French prisoners, shot and shell meanwhile pouring into
them. The hardest heart must have recoiled from this scene of
horror; wounded men being rewounded, many of whom had
received previously the most frightful injuries. Here a man
with an arm suspended only by a single muscle, another with
his head horribly mangled by a sabre cut, or one with half his
face shot away, received fresh damage.

Lieutenant George Simmons of the 95th Rifles had been wounded when a musket ball penetrated his back, broke two ribs, passed

The farm of Mont St Jean about a decade after the battle. (ASKB)

Mont St Jean Farm today.

The Prince of Orange is wounded in the shoulder towards the end of the battle, at the point where the Lion Mound now stands. (ASKB)

through his liver and lodged in his breast. He was taken back to the farm of Mont St Jean, where the ball was cut out by a surgeon. But he fainted as he was being put on a horse to take him further to the rear and when he came to, he overheard the surgeons saying:

> *What is the use of torturing him? He cannot live the night;*
> *he is better where he is than to die on horseback.*

Yet cannonballs were striking the farm and it seemed as if the French might break through at any moment, so Simmons was

A watercolour showing the type of injuries a surgeon had to face at Waterloo.

again put on a horse, this time successfully, and he set off northwards to Brussels. He later recalled:

Oh what I suffered, I had to ride twelve miles. The motion of the horse made the blood pump out, and the bones cut the flesh to a jelly.

At Brussels, he eventually made a full recovery against the odds, and died in 1858 aged seventy-two.

Medical attention was crude and primitive. A common treatment was to bleed the patient, either with leeches or the knife. In many such cases, modern medics would do the exact opposite and administer a blood transfusion. To prevent gangrene, wounded limbs were generally amputated without anaesthetics, which were then unknown. Even so, most soldiers bore the excruciating pain of such operations with incredible fortitude: one plucky Frenchman seized his amputated leg and tossed it in the air with a shout of 'Long live the Emperor!' As for Lord Fitzroy Somerset, he was so unshaken that he called out: 'Hallo! don't carry away that arm till I've taken off my ring.' Other joked about the blunt saw their surgeon was using: 'Take your time, Mr Carver.'

One of the cruellest tasks of the surgeons, wrote William Gibney,

was to be obliged to tell a dying soldier who had served his king and country well on that day, that his case was hopeless, more especially when he was unable to realise the same for himself, and then to pass on to another, where skill might avail.

The most famous amputation was that of the leg of Wellington's cavalry commander, Lieutenant-General the Earl of Uxbridge. He was struck by one of the last shots of the battle when riding alongside Wellington and promptly exclaimed, 'By God, sir, I've lost my leg!' Wellington is said to have glanced down at the mangled limb, murmured 'By God, sir, so you have,' and resumed his scutiny of the battlefield through his telescope. Whatever the truth of this celebrated exchange, Wellington in fact supported Uxbridge in the saddle until assistance arrived. Uxbridge was

Lieutenant-General the Earl of Uxbridge. (ASKB)

105

then taken northwards to the village of Waterloo where his leg was amputated in the house of Monsieur Hyacinthe Paris, at 214 Chaussée de Bruxelles. He made no sound during the operation and it was noted that his nerves and pulse were afterwards unshaken.

Uxbridge was created Marquis of Anglesey in recognition of his courage, while Monsieur Paris had the severed leg placed in a tomb in his garden with a flowery inscription. An English visitor is said to have scribbed another couple of lines: 'Here lies the Marquis of Anglesey's limb; The Devil will have the remainder of him.' Another version reads: 'Here lies the Marquis of Anglesey's leg; Pray for the rest of his body, I beg.' The tomb was transferred to the grounds of the Wellington Museum in March 1991 as it was impossible to preserve it in its original location.

It would have been impossible to cope with the sheer numbers of wounded had it not been for the local habitants, who helped care for some of the injured in their own homes and generously donated bedding and blankets and old linen for making bandages. The medical personnel attached to the armies were pitifully few in number, but included skilled and dedicated men, among them, the most famous military surgeon of the age, the Frenchman Dominique Larrey. They were aided by civilian surgeons, including some who travelled from Britain to offer their services. Among these was Charles Bell, who wrote of the amputations he performed in Brussels:

> It was a strange thing to feel my clothes stiff with blood, and my arms powerless with the exertion of using a knife! and more extraordinary still, to find my mind calm amidst such variety of suffering; but to give one of these objects access to your feelings was to allow yourself to be unmanned for the performance of a duty. It was less painful to look upon the whole than to contemplate one object.

It was small wonder that Wellington broke down in tears when he heard the list of his casualties, 'I hope to God that I have fought my last battle.' He remarked a few weeks later:

> It is a bad thing to be always fighting. While I am in the thick of it I am too much occupied to feel anything; but it is wretched just after. It is quite impossible to think of glory ... I always say that, next to a battle lost, the greatest misery is a battle gained.

WEAPONS AND TACTICS

The weapons used at Waterloo were remarkably inefficient compared with those of today. The infantryman's basic weapon was the flintlock musket, which fired when a flint snapped against a steel frizzen and produced a spark that ignited the powder charge inside the barrel through a touch-hole. Not surprisingly, these primitive weapons often misfired, particularly in damp weather, and quickly became fouled with burnt powder. They also had to be loaded by ramming a cartridge down the barrel from the muzzle, which limited the rate of fire to barely two shots a minute.

The muskets were smooth-bores, which meant that the inside of the barrels had no rifling to spin the bullet as it was fired. As a consequence, they were barely accurate at 80 yards. Paradoxically, this inaccuracy made for murderous actions, for troops had to form up in tightly-packed ranks and fire together in massed volleys in order to compensate for the inadequacies of individual weapons. It is small wonder that the concentrated effect of muskets and cannon at close range was horrendous.

The French infantry attack

Throughout the battle, French infantry tended to advance in heavy columns, or blocks of troops. These columns varied in size, but their width occupied a greater distance than their depth. Such columns were used because they were the easiest formation in which to manoeuvre large numbers of troops. They looked formidable and could advance quickly without losing their cohesion, but had limited firepower, for only the front three ranks could fire without hitting their comrades in front. The French commanders therefore intended, when they came up to their opponents, to deploy their columns into longer and thinner lines to boost their firepower. The problem was to know when to deploy.

To meet a French infantry attack, Wellington would deploy his British battalions into lines about 150 yards long and two ranks deep, so that every soldier could bring his musket to

107

Tower musket (the British Brown Bess).

bear. He would keep his troops hidden on the reverse slopes of his ridge, where they were sheltered from artillery fire. When the French columns came up, the British would advance to the ridge crest, surprise them, shatter them with a volley or two as they vainly tried to deploy, and then complete their overthrow with a bayonet charge.

The Square

Infantry threatened by cavalry would quickly form a hollow oblong, or 'square', with each side usually four ranks deep. The outer two ranks knelt or crouched and presented a thick hedge of bayonets, while the inner two ranks blasted the horsemen with volleys. These squares allowed all-round defence and were practically impregnable to unsupported cavalry. However, they were vulnerable to artillery fire since, unlike the thin line, they

French cuirassiers attacking a British infantry square. (ASKB)

108

Napoleon and his Imperial Guard. (ASKB)

concentrated large numbers of troops in a small area.

Skirmishers

Although most infantrymen fought in tightly-packed formations, some did fight in open-order, as skirmishers. These swarms of light infantrymen ran about and sniped at enemy units in order to shake them up and pick off their officers. A few allied skirmishing units, such as the British 95th Rifles (now part of the Royal Green Jackets), carried rifles, which were accurate at about twice the range of the musket but were slower to load. Because skirmishers fought in open order, they were vulnerable to cavalry, but difficult to hit with musketry or artillery fire.

Cavalry

Cavalry consisted of two types: heavy and light. The powerful heavies, for example cuirassiers and heavy dragoons, excelled at battlefield charges. The light cavalry, such as hussars and lancers, were used in particular for reconnaissance and outpost duties. Charges tended to be made at a fast trot rather than an all-out gallop, so that the ranks did not lose their cohesion: maintaining momentum was more important than speed.

Artillery

The artillery had muzzle-loading, smooth-bore guns, which were inaccurate but murderous at close range and terrifying when used in massed batteries. They were slow to load (a maximum of three shots per minute) and the British artillery fired an average of only 129 rounds per gun during the battle. All the guns were drawn by teams of horses before being unlimbered

British heavy cavalry charging French guns. (ASKB)

and placed in their firing positions. Most were 6, 9 and 12-pounder cannon, which fired roundshot directly at the foe and hence had to be placed in the front line. The recoil after each shot meant that the weary gunners repeatedly had to heave the heavy gun back into its original position.

The heavier guns had greater range and hitting power, but even the 12-pounder, the heaviest cannon on the battlefield, had an effective range of only about 1000 yards. The lighter guns were more mobile. All armies also had howitzers, which lobbed shells in a high arc; these projectiles, iron spheres filled with gunpowder, exploded after landing thanks to a fuse lit by the firing of the gun. At close range, both cannon and howitzers also fired canister, a tin can filled with scores of lead balls. When the gun fired, the can burst, causing its contents to scythe down whole ranks of enemy troops. The British artillery had two additional weapons. The first was shrapnel: shells that burst in the air and showered the enemy below with the balls that had been packed inside. The second was the primitive and notoriously erratic Congreve rocket, which only one battery used at Waterloo: it had a long stabilising stick and was armed with either a roundshot or an exploding warhead.

Tactics

The key to good tactics was to co-ordinate infantry, cavalry and artillery, so that each arm supported the other. One reason for the French defeat was that they failed to do this until the evening, by which time they lacked the strength to achieve a breakthrough. For most of the battle, they simply attacked with massive infantry columns or with unsupported cavalry.

Communications

There were no radio communications at the time of Waterloo and so commanders had to rely on mounted messengers, who often arrived late, if at all. The clouds of smoke produced by the firearms soon made it difficult to see what was happening, but the inaccuracy of the muskets made it possible for generals to command from the front line (as Wellington did) without being picked off by enemy marksmen.

Uniforms

Similarly, inaccurate firearms made camouflage unnecessary. Armies today wear drab, standardized colours, but Waterloo was one of the greatest pageants of history, with troops wearing the

Re-enactments are held every five years to commemorate the battle. These are Grenadiers of Napoleon's Imperial Guard.

French infantry re-enactors.

most elaborate and colourful uniforms imaginable. As a rule, British infantry wore red, with the notable exception of the green-coated 95th Rifles. In contrast, the Prussians wore particularly diverse uniforms, including items looted from the French or supplied by the British. One result of this confusing kaleidoscope of colour was that it was often difficult to tell friend from foe and this contributed to many tragic incidents of friendly fire in the heat of the battle.

TIPS FOR TOURISTS

For museum opening times and other up-to-date information, contact this Tourist Information Office: S.I. Waterloo, Chaussée de Bruxelles 149, 1410 Waterloo, Belgium. Alternatively, check out the following website:

www.waterloo.org.

If you intend to visit all the battlefield museums, buy a *ticket commun*, which offers combined entry at a discount to all of these attractions: the Visitors' Centre, Lion Mound, Panorama, Waxworks Museum, Wellington Museum and Le Caillou.

Please respect the privacy and property of the local farmers. Remember that the ground, including La Haie Sainte, Hougoumont and the other historic farms, is in private hands. Please stay on the roads and major tracks.

Re-enactments of the battle normally take place around the

British Royal Horse Artillery re-enactors in action.

113

anniversary (18 June) every five years. These spectacular events feature thousands of re-enactors in studiously authentic uniforms, plus sound-and-light shows.

More monuments are likely to be erected on the battlefield in the run up to the 200th anniversary of Waterloo in 2015. Plans under consideration include a new tourist complex at the Lion Mound.

If time permits, you may wish to visit the other battlefields of the 1815 campaign: Quatre Bras, Ligny and Wavre. They all have memorials to the soldiers who died there and Ligny also has a small museum.

If you are staying in Brussels, be sure to visit the Belgian Army Museum, which contains some fascinating Waterloo relics. You should also visit the Evere cemetery in the north-eastern suburbs of Brussels, where you can see the impressive memorial to the British soldiers who fell in the campaign.

Napoleon's Imperial Guard: re-enactors on the battlefield.

FURTHER READING

Hundreds of books have been written about Waterloo and we don't want to overwhelm you with an unendurable list of references. However, if you are interested in learning more about the battle, we would suggest that you start with these readable factual works:

Brett-James, Antony, *The hundred days* (1964)

Chalfont, Lord, ed., *Waterloo: battle of three armies* (1979)

Chandler, David, *Waterloo: the hundred days* (1980; reissued 1998)

Haythornthwaite, Philip, *Uniforms of Waterloo* (1974; reissued 1996)

Hofschröer, Peter, *1815 the Waterloo campaign: the German victory* (1999)

Howarth, David, *A near run thing* (1968; reissued 1998)

Keegan, John, *The face of battle* (1976; reissued 1998)

Longford, Lady Elizabeth, *Wellington: the years of the sword* (1969; reissued with its sequel, *Wellington: pillar of state*, in 1992 as an abridged one volume edition)

Mercer, Cavalié, *Journal of the Waterloo campaign* (1870; reissued 1995)

Nofi, Albert, *The Waterloo campaign, June 1815* (1993; reissued 1998)

Siborne, Herbert, ed., *The Waterloo letters* (1891; reissued 1993)

Uffindell, Andrew, *The eagle's last triumph: Napoleon's victory at Ligny, June 1815* (1994)

Uffindell, Andrew and Corum, Michael, *On the fields of glory: the battlefields of the 1815 campaign* (1996; reissued 2002)

Weller, Jac, *Wellington at Waterloo* (1967; reissued 1998)

Weller, Jac, *On Wellington: the Duke and his art of war* (1998)

You may also like to try three superb historical novels:

Cornwell, Bernard, *Sharpe's Waterloo* (1990)

Heyer, Georgette, *An infamous army* (1937; reissued 1992)

Hugo, Victor, *Les Misérables* (1862; reissued 1998)

ACKNOWLEDGEMENTS

Pictures annotated ASKB were reproduced with the kind permission of the Anne S.K. Brown Military Collection at Brown University Library in Providence, Rhode Island, USA. We are grateful to Lionel Leventhal for permission to reproduce the diagrams of Hougoumont, which were published in *On the fields of glory: the battlefields of the 1815 campaign* (Greenhill Books, 1996).

We are also indebted to John Richards for drawing the superb maps included in this guidebook.

The authors and publishers have done their best to ensure the accuracy of all the information in this book; however, they can accept no responsibility for any loss, injury or inconvenience sustained by any traveller as a result of information or advice contained in this book.

Waterloo was Napoleon's final and most famous defeat. It brought peace to Europe after more than two decades of war and was one of the most decisive battles of history.

Despite the passage of time, Waterloo has lost none of its fascination and attracts thousands of visitors from around the world. This guidebook is the first in an exciting new series designed to help you discover the Waterloo campaign. These readable books are filled with maps, diagrams and photographs to enable you to follow the dramatic events on the ground as they actually happened. The authors quote eyewitnesses to bring alive the incidents that occurred at the various points of interest.

Look out for forthcoming titles on the principal commanders and their armies, as well as the preliminary battles of Quatre Bras and Ligny.

Andrew Uffindell and Michael Corum are freelance writers from Britain and the United States. They have written extensively on military history and are the authors of the critically-acclaimed *On the fields of glory: the battlefields of the 1815 campaign.*

INDEX